THE LITTLE PRINCESS

CASSANDRA GAISFORD

PRAISE FOR THE LITTLE PRINCESS

"A Beautiful and Life Changing Message…
This book shares a powerful message for all women of any age, I wish I had this when I was growing up. Today more than ever, we have to stay true to ourselves, follow our Spirit and do the work we're here to do - amidst disapproval and criticism. The simple steps in this book will guide your way, and help you to navigate through the confusion, uncertainty, and inner blocks, so you live your one precious life in a big way."

~ **Vesna Hrsto, Naturopath and Coach**

"A Little Book with a Powerful Message...
An important reminder to always be true to yourself

and summon the courage to follow your passions...
Only *you* can live your life...GO live it!"

~ **Harley**

"The Little Princess is my hero...
I am a Midlife Coach, which means I help women find their moxie to do what they might not have done in the first half of their lives...I think *The Little Princess* needs to be a "required reading" text book for us all...she cuts to the heart of the lesson all of us need to hear, over and over again. *The Little Princess* embodies courage. She is my hero."

~ **Sheree Clark, Midlife Courage Coach**

"The Little Princess **is 'brilliant...**
Short concise & full of tremendous vision & wisdom, expressed lovingly. Many of the comments read true for my own journey. I recognise my passion to be different than many others, my persistence to succeed, & the pure joy I have at the end of each day when I lay down my head & give thanks."

~ **Kenn Butler, CEO**

"Very uplifting and inspiring…
I love everything Cassandra writes, the queen of uplifting inspiration! This is a little book, the story basically teaches you to have faith in your dreams, stand firm and don't let others rain on your parade.. We are all searching for purpose and passion, everybody hurts and sometimes we find ourselves on the receiving end of somebody else's insecurities, when they project their anger, jealousy etc onto us.. The old woman who puts the little princess down is really just jealous and stuck in her own life."

~ **Reviewer UK**

"A reminder of the truth in all of us…
The Little Princess is a great short story as a reminder of the truth in all of us; Don't judge, take loving kindness as a guideline in life, but stay true to yourself; A powerful message! Like all the books by this author, it is a guideline to live a wise life."

~ **Maartje Jager, Designer**

DEDICATION

*I dedicate this book to those
who have inspired ideas,
and the courage to do what others may say cannot
be done.*

ABOUT THE BOOK

From the bestselling author of *I Have to Grow* comes a brilliant new series, *Transformational Super Kid*s.

These modern-day heroes and heroines tackle modern-day problems with the passion and gusto of warriors.

They defeat cruel critics, they slay savage self-esteem demons, and they show people—jealous of their kindness, talent, and beauty—that their biggest superpower is staying true to themselves.

Suitable for 'kids' of all ages—aren't we all children at heart?

1

*O*nce upon a time there was a young woman who wanted to make a difference in the world.

She wanted to help others. She wanted to help people overcome depression, anxiety, and feeling sad.

She wanted to help them feel inspired, joyful and happy.

She just wasn't sure how.

2

*O*ne day she had an inspired idea. "I can help people find their passion and purpose," she thought.

Her heart fluttered then soared higher and higher and higher—far, far, far away.

Almost beyond the reach of her doubts and fears.

3

She felt so excited—but also scared. She decided to feel the fear and create something anyway.

She knew people often struggled to find the time to read, and she wanted to make it easy and fun for people to find inspiration and help.

She decided to design a pack of inspirational cards that would enable people to help themselves and become empowered to transform their lives.

The cards would give people ideas, encourage them to dream, and give them hope.

4

She thought about the angel cards that had given her so much relief when she was an anxious child.

"Wouldn't it be fun to create something similar?" she thought.

Each card would have an inspirational quote on one side and a self-help strategy on the other.

5

It sounded easy. But it wasn't. She quickly discovered that writing less words and distilling ideas into something short and sweet, took way longer than a long and lengthy book.

She realised that to touch peoples hearts you had to find exactly the right words.

6

One day she was invited by a friend to a dinner party. "What do you do?" a guest, who was a nurse, asked.

It wasn't an easy thing to answer because the young woman did many things to earn her living.

"At the moment I'm developing a set of cards to

help people find their passion and purpose," she replied, quietly.

"People like you make me sick," the older woman spat.

7

*H*er words were like spears.

The young woman felt her face burn and her chest burst. She didn't know what to say. She went into shock.

"What makes you think you can go around telling people what to do?" the older woman hissed.

"I'm not," the younger woman stammered, her voice a squeak. "I'm just trying to help people. They don't have to read it if they don't want to."

The older woman glared at her. "My, aren't we a little princess."

8

The angry nurse sat rigidly in her chair like an ice queen, dispensing her frosty displeasure.

"You write a column in the newspaper. You're public property. You should expect criticism."

The young woman went to defend herself—then pressed her lips firmly shut.

Suddenly she realised what was going on. The nurse felt jealous and envious and resentful.

But rather than respond unkindly, the young woman felt sorry for her. She felt her pain.

She realised that the nurse was showing her wounds.

9

*T*he young woman studied the nurse and looked beyond her harsh, stony, indignant facade.

She looked beyond her offensive, insulting and unjust accusations.

She looked beyond her livid, irate, and scornful face.

But, more importantly, the young woman saw mirrored in the older woman's eyes the young woman's own need to please.

She saw her own need to have people like her.

She saw her own need to be accepted.

10

*H*appy people don't attack others, the young woman reminded herself. Happy people don't talk like this.

The little princess suddenly felt grateful for what the nurse was teaching her.

The little princess knew she would never be able

to find and honour her soul purpose if she kept trying to please others.

The little princess would never be true to herself if she feared disapproval.

The little princess would never share her gifts and talents and passion with the world if she stayed small and showed no courage.

11

*A*nd the little princess knew she would never help others if she let the nurse, or anyone else's criticism, stop her from doing things that made her soul sing.

She had to follow her dreams.
She had to live her passion.
She had to fill her life with purpose.

Thank you, the little princess said to the older woman, silently. Thank you for the gift you have given me.

"I guess, we'll just have to agree to disagree," the little princess said, happily.

*** THE END ***

EPILOGUE

"I'm sorry," said the nurse. "I've been rude." She looked down and studied her hands, then she looked up. "It's just, well, I just feel like I've never accomplished anything in my life."

The little princess bit her lip, resisting the urge to say something to make the nurse feel better. Far better to let her speak, she decided. Far kinder to listen to her story.

The nurse told the little princess of the dreams she'd never followed. She told the little princess of the fears that kept her stuck. She told the little princess how her life was full of regrets.

She told her that she had been jealous and how hearing the little princess talk about following her dreams had made her feel inadequate.

She told her everything she wanted to say. And the little princess just listened.

Then at last the nurse said, "Thank you. Thank you for inspiring me to stop making excuses and to get on with my life."

AUTHOR'S NOTE

The Little Princess was inspired by a true story. You may have already guessed that—especially if you have purchased *The Passion Pack* or read my bestselling book, *How to Find Your Passion and Purpose: Four Easy Steps to Discover A Job You Want And Live the Life You Love.*

I learned so much from my experience in the wake of the other woman's attack. I learned to stay true to myself, and realised that there were always going to be people who didn't like what I did or who I was.

It would have been easy to be stopped in my tracks. It would have been easy to stay small. It would have been easy to have done nothing at all.

But then what sort of life would I have had?

Creating *The Passion Pack* and writing *How to Find Your Passion and Purpose* opened so many doors and galaxies for me.

So many people have written to me and told me how those cards and that book changed their lives. It continues to change mine.

Importantly, my experience that night so many moons ago, made me realise that finding our passion and purpose is not simply about being inspired.

It's also knowing how to conquer obstacles. Sometimes it's not possible to obliterate the things that block our path. What's important is the determination not to let barriers stand in our way.

I hope by sharing my story, you realise how wonderful it is to be a little princess. Isn't that every girl's dream!

I'm so excited to let you know that *The Little Princess* will soon be available as an audiobook—narrated by me! Subscribe to my newsletter and follow me on social media to be the first to know when it's released.

Read on for a short poem called The Loving Tree and a wee excerpt from the second book in this series—*I Have to Grow*—it's inspired by my beautiful, kind daughter Hannah Joy. I released the book just in time for her 28th birthday on the 27th of May 2019!

Read on also for an excerpt from my bestselling book *How to Find Your Passion and Purpose.* I've included some of my favourite chapters. Please note these aren't in the order that they appear in the book.

Follow your bliss dear readers—don't let anyone stop you from sharing your passion and purpose with the world.

MUCH LOVE

THE LOVING TREE

The oak tree grows toward the light
The gnarly cypress towers above
Pushing against the oak, stunting its might
The oak stands its ground
Its roots arch and spread and burrow

Down, down, down it grows
Down, down, down it goes
Down, down, down it reaches

Seeking water
Seeking nourishment
Seeking Mother Earth

Up, up, up it reaches
Up, up, up it goes
Up, up, up it grows

Its branches arch and spread and borrows
Borrows the energy of the earth and sky
Borrows the whispers of the wind
Borrows the song of the birds
Borrows the comforting touch of those just like her

And she grows where she can
And she stands her ground
And she flourishes and thrives
And she lets go of that which has died

And she knows
Yes, she knows
She *really* knows

That what she releases is past
And there will be a time to weep
A time to cry
A time to say goodbye

And she will rest
She will sleep
And then one day
Again, she shall meet
The little seeds of hope so sweet
And the tiny buds of dormant growth
Will in a whisper unfurl

And the growth will be new
And the growth will be vital
And the growth will delight

This is nature
This is natural
This is how magic happens

And who knows what tomorrow will bring
Every day is another opportunity
To start again
And bloom.

EXCERPT: I HAVE TO GROW

PRAISE FOR I HAVE TO GROW

"Courageous, compassionate and inspiring…
Courage is more than just standing up for yourself or doing hard things—it's doing so with compassion. Little Hannah is courageous, compassionate, talented and inspiring!"

~ Sheree Clarke, Midlife Courage Coach

"Such a powerful message.…
This is a splendid little book for any person aspiring to reach another level, with such a powerful message. Of never, ever listening to anyone who steals your light. Cassandra is a shining example of turning every situation, including setbacks, into learning & growing opportunities.

As one who has taken advantage of the wisdom, knowledge & ability of Cassandra, to communicate, over a number of years, I would encourage you to read this book thoroughly & think deeply on your own situation.

For her daughter Hannah, with the voice of an angel & heart of God, you have indeed been blessed."

~ Kenn Butler, CEO

1

*L*ittle Hannah was happily singing on her swing, when Little Angie went by.

"You think you can sing but you can't," she shouted.

Little Hannah stopped singing and ran inside.

2

"What's wrong?" Big Cassie asked as Little Hannah ran crying to her room.

"Little Angie is being mean to me," she sobbed. "She says I can't sing."

3

"Little Angie is just jealous!" Big Cassie told Little Hannah, giving her a cuddle.

"You have a beautiful voice. Promise me you'll always sing—no matter what."

DID YOU ENJOY THIS EXCERPT?

Sing Your Song! Heed the Call for Courage

Feeling discouraged, bullied, sabotaged or held back?

Part moral allegory and part spiritual biography, *I Have to Grow* is a timeless charm which tells the story of a young girl who leaves the security of playing small, to follow her heart and heal the world.

Little Hannah, is a beautiful and kind-hearted child, with a very special voice. When the cruel and jealous Angie tries to rob Little Hannah of her gifts she believes the answer is to stay small. But, things go from bad to worse.

Bullied and taunted Little Hannah doesn't stand

much of a chance. Until a magical creature appears and encourages her to stand tall and shine like a star.

Liberate the music you have inside. Share your voice.

Life is about learning to follow your inner voice, live your truth and share your gifts. It is also about reclaiming your power, not hanging back, playing second best and being discouraged.

Find and cherish your unique abilities and raise your voice to the heavens.

Reconnect with your magnificent soul self and don't allow self-doubt or the envy of others to hold you back—you will reach your potential.

There are so many reasons why you should *follow your dreams*. **If you need some inspiration, look no further than this book.**

Be inspired by this journey to transformation and self-acceptance, and self-belief as our heroine learns to overcome the vagaries of child and adult behaviour. Her personal odyssey culminates in a voyage of self-belief, passion, and purpose.

From the best-selling author of *Mid-Life Career Rescue*, *Stress Less*, *How to Find Your Passion and Purpose,* and *The Little Princess*: a powerful, inspiring, and practical book about boosting

Did you enjoy this excerpt?

resilience, overcoming obstacles, finding courage and moving forward after life's inevitable setbacks.

Find out who and what is sabotaging your success. Find and follow your passion and purpose faster.

Bonus: Free Excerpts from *The Little Princess* and *How to Find Your Passion and Purpose*—overcome common obstacles to success easily (focus on your strengths, use anger constructively, follow your inspiration—and other clues.)

Available in Audio, eBook,Paperback, and Hardback from all great online retailers.

EXCERPT: HOW TO FIND YOUR PASSION AND PURPOSE

**PRAISE FOR HOW TO FIND YOUR
PASSION AND PURPOSE**

"This little book on a BIG topic that resonates with me packs a lot of wisdom that is worth investing time in. Cassandra challenges us to "Dare to Dream!" Take the time and make the effort to find the work you feel passionate about; You could read this in less than two hours and be on your way to sculpting out a new way of living if you're not living your passionate lifestyle yet."

**~ Scott.B. Allan, Author of #1
bestseller *Empower Your Thoughts***

"This excellent little book is quick to read but left me with much to think about and many practical steps to take to find my passion and incorporate it into my life. There are several free resources to download which increase the worth of this already very valuable book."

~ Jenny Cliff, Author of *The Music Inside*

"*How to Find Your Passion and Purpose* is a positive and enabling companion and offers much. It encourages us to identify our passion and interests, to live from our core values and use our signature strengths creatively. It highlights that it's never too late to make changes, to get on the path of true fulfillment and make a living. Dig into this book and let Cassandra be your guide, inspiration and coach as she calls forth your creativity and gives practical steps to take you where you need to go next. Step into this ride joyfully and create your future."

~ Jasbindar Singh, Business Psychologist and Author of *Get Your Groove Back*

AUTHOR'S NOTE

This book is a concise guide to making the most of your life. It began its journey some years ago as *The Passion Pack* – a set of 40 cards created to help people live and work with passion.

The vision was simple: a few short, easy to digest tips for time-challenged people who were looking for inspiration and practical strategies to encourage positive change.

From my own experience, I knew that people didn't need a large wad of words to feel inspired, gain clarity and be stimulated to take action.

In coaching and counselling sessions I'd encourage my clients to ask a question they would like answered. The questions could be specific, such as, 'How can I make a living from my passion?' Or vague, for example, 'What do I most need to know?'

Then I'd ask them to pick a card at random. Without fail, they were astounded by the card's potent relevance. Disbelieving eyes widened in astonishment as they read either the quote or the main message they received. Many would say, "These cards are magic."

Orders flooded in from global recruitment consultancies, primary schools, colleges, universities, not-for-profit organizations, financial institutions and other multi-national commercial entities. I was asked to speak at conferences around the world about the power of passion. It was amazing to see how popular and successful *The Passion Pack* became, transcending age, gender, and socio-economic differences.

In this era of information obesity the need for simple, life-affirming messages is even more important. If you are looking for inspiration and practical tips, in short, sweet sound bites, this guide is for you.

Similarly, if you are a grazer, or someone more methodical, this guide will also work for you. Pick a page at random, or work through the steps sequentially. I encourage you to experiment, be open-minded and try new things. I promise you will achieve outstanding results.

Clive, a 62-year-old man who had suffered work-related burnout, did! He thought that creating a passion journal, *Tip 10* in this guide, was childish – something other stressed executives in his men's support group would balk at. But once he'd taken up the challenge he told me enthusiastically,

"They loved it!" They are using their passion journals to visualize, gain clarity, and create their preferred futures. Clive is using it to help manifest his new purpose-driven coaching business.

Let experience be your guide. Give your brain a well-needed break. Let go of 'why', and embrace how you *feel*, or how you want to feel. Honor the messages from your intuition and follow your path with heart.

Laura, who at one stage seemed rudderless career-wise, did just that. She was guided to *Tip 14: Who Inspires You?* Following that, her motivation to live and work like those she looked up to sparked a determination to start her own business. It was that simple.

At the time of writing I've just turned to Tip *31:*

Fear Of Success. It's a timely reminder of just how far following my passion has taken me – the shy girl who was once afraid of being seen. The quote is as apt for me as I feel it may be for you:

"Your playing small doesn't serve the world."

Here's to living with passion and purpose!

INTRODUCTION

"Mary Oliver says in one of her poems, 'Tell me, what is it that you plan to do with your one wild and precious life?' Me, I intend to live passionately."
Isabel Allende, Novelist

Finding a job you want and living a life you love is impossible without passion, enthusiasm, zest, inspiration and the deep satisfaction that comes from doing something that delivers you some kind of buzz.

Yet, it's staggeringly, and dishearteningly, true that many people don't know what they are passionate about, or how they can turn it into a rewarding career. Some research suggests that only

10% of people are living and working with passion. Hence my passion for passion and helping create more positive change in the world.

If you're like many people who don't know what they are passionate about or what gives your life meaning and purpose, this book will help provide the answers.

If you have been told it's not realistic to work and live with passion, this book will help change your mindset.

Together we'll help you get your mojo back, challenge your current beliefs and increase your sense of possibility. By tapping into a combination of practical career strategies, Law of Attraction principles, and the spiritual powers of manifestation, you'll reawaken dreams, boost your self-awareness, empower your life and challenge what you thought was possible.

We'll do this in an inspired yet structured way by strengthening your creative thinking skills, boosting your self-awareness and helping you identify your non-negotiable ingredients for career success and happiness. Little steps will lead naturally to bigger leaps, giving you the courage and confidence to follow your passion and fly free towards career happiness and life fulfilment.

What you're about to read isn't another self-help book; it's a self-empowerment book. It offers ways to increase your self-knowledge. From that knowledge comes the power to create a life worth living.

How to Find Your Passion and Purpose will help you:

- Explore and clarify your passions, interests, and life purpose
- Build a strong foundation for happiness and success
- Value your gifts, and talents and confirm your work-related strengths
- Direct your energies positively toward your preferred future
- Strengthen your creative thinking skills, and ability to identify possible roles you would enjoy, including self-employment
- Have the courage to follow your dreams and super-charge the confidence needed to make an inspired change
- Find your point of brilliance

Let's look briefly at what each chapter in this book will cover:

Step One, "The Call For Passion" will help

you explore the meaning of passion and discover the benefits of following it, and consequences of ignoring your passion. You'll identify any passion blocking beliefs and intensify passion-building beliefs to boost your chances of success.

Step Two, "Discover Your Passion," will help you to identify your own sources of passion and passion criteria. What you'll discover may be a complete surprise and open up a realm of opportunities you've never considered.

Step Three, "Passion at Work," will assist you in identifying career options and exploring ways to develop your career in light of your passions and life purpose.

Step Four, "Live Your Passion," looks at passion beyond the world of work and ways to achieve greater balance and fulfilment. You'll also identify strategies to overcome obstacles and to maximise your success.

How to Find Your Passion and Purpose concludes with showing you how to identify your point of brilliance.

How To Use This Book—Your Virtual Coach

To really benefit from this book think of it as your 'virtual' coach—answer the questions and complete the additional exercises that you'll find in the chapters and free extras.

Questions are great thought provokers. Your answers to these questions will help you gently challenge current assumptions and gain greater clarity about your goals and desires.

All the strategies are designed to facilitate greater insight and to help you integrate new learnings. Resist the urge to just process information in your head. We learn best by doing. Research has repeatedly proven that the act of writing deepens your knowledge and understanding.

For example, a study conducted by Dr. David K. Pugalee, found that journal writing was an effective instructional tool and aided learning. His research found that writing helped people organize and describe internal thoughts and thus improve their problem solving-skills.

Henriette Klauser, Ph.D., also provides compelling evidence in her book, *Write It Down and Make It Happen*, that writing helps you clarify what you want and enables you to make it happen.

Writing down your insights is the area where people like motivational guru Tony Robbins, say that the winners part from the losers, because the losers always find a reason not to write things down. Harsh but perhaps true!

Keeping A Passion Journal

A passion journal is also a great place to store sources of inspiration to support you through the career planning and change process. For some tips to help you create your own inspirational passion journal, go to the media page on my website and watch my television interview and interview with other experts here:

http://www.cassandragaisford.com/media

This Book Is Magical

This book proves less really is more. Sometimes all it takes to radically transform your life is one word, one sentence, one powerful but simple strategy to ignite inspiration and reawaken a sense of possibility.

I have successfully used the knowledge I'm sharing with you in this book professionally with my clients and personally during numerous reinventions.

I stand by every one of the 4 steps and the 40+ strategies you will learn here, not just because they are grounded in strong evidence-based, scientific and spiritual principles, but also because I have successfully used them to create turnaround, after turnaround in nearly every area of my life.

How to Find Your Passion and Purpose is the culmination of all that I have experienced and all that I have learned, applied and taught others for over two decades. I don't practice what I preach; I preach what I have practiced—because it gets results.

Why Did I Write This Book?

If you are curious about *The Passion Pack* and why I created *How To Find Your Passion and Purpose*, you may like to check out my blog post here:

http://www.cassandragaisford.com/2557-2/

Setting You Up For Success

"Aren't you setting people up for failure?" a disillusioned career coach once challenged me.

Twenty-five years of cumulative professional experience as a career coach and counsellor, helping people work with passion and still pay the bills, answers that question. I'm setting people up for success. I'm not saying it will happen instantly, but if you follow the advice in this book, it will happen. I promise.

I've proven repeatedly, both personally and professionally, that thinking differently and creatively, rationally and practically, while also harnessing the power of your heart, and applying the principles of manifestation, really works. In this book, I'll show you why—and how.

A large part of my philosophy and the reason behind my success with clients is my fervent belief that to achieve anything worthy of life you need to follow your passion. And I'm in good company.

As media giant Oprah Winfrey once said, "Passion is energy. Feel the power that comes from focusing on what excites you."

Passion's Pay Cheque

By discovering your passion and purpose you will tap into a huge source of potential energy and prosperity. Pursuing your passion can be profitable on many levels:

- When you do what you love, your true talent will reveal itself; passion can't be faked

- You'll be more enthusiastic about your pursuits
- You'll have more energy to overcome obstacles
- You will be more determined to make things happen
- You will enjoy your work
- Your work will become a vehicle for self-expression
- Passion will give you a competitive edge
- You'll enjoy your life and magnetize positive experiences toward you

Without passion, you don't have energy, and without energy you have nothing.

You have to let love, desire, and passion, not fear or ambivalence or apathy, propel you forward. Yet worryingly, research suggests that less than 10% of people are following their passion. Perhaps that's why there is so much unhappiness in the world.

Don't waste another day feeling uninspired. Don't be the person who spends a life of regret, or waits until they retire before they follow their passions, be you. Don't be the person too afraid to make a change for the better, or who wishes they could lead a significant life. Make the change now. Before it's too late.

Extra Support: Companion Workbook

How to Find Your Passion and Purpose (the book) offers you information about overcoming adversity, building resilience and finding joy. Reading a book is great but applying the teachings and writing things down in a dedicated space helps bring the learning alive, deepens your self awareness, and enables you to make real world change. Reading gives you knowledge, but reflecting upon and applying that knowledge creates true empowerment.

By writing and recording your responses you're rewriting the story of your life. As Seth Godin states, "Here's the thing: The book that will most change your life is the book you write. The act of writing things down, of justifying your actions, of being cogent and clear, and forthright—that's how you change."

The *How to Find Your Passion and Purpose Companion Workbook* will support you through the learning and show you how to create real and meaningful change in your life...simply and joyfully.

Reach For Your Dreams

Passion, happiness, joy, fulfilment, love—call it what you will, my deepest desire is that this book encourages you to reach for your dreams, to never settle, to believe in the highest aspirations you have for yourself.

You have so many gifts, so many talents that the world so desperately needs. We need people like you who care about what they do, who want to live and work with passion and purpose.

I promise that if you follow the steps in this book you'll discover what you really want to do, clarify what you can do, and create powerful but simple strategies to make your dream a reality. You'll find a job that you love, one that adds more joy to your life and gives you a sense of meaning, purpose, and fulfilment.

And what I can promise you is this—whatever your circumstances, it's never too late to re-create yourself and your life. So, what are you waiting for?

Let's get started!

STEP 1: THE CALL FOR PASSION

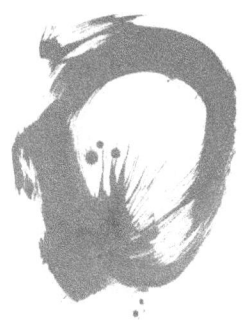

Read through the following tips numbered 1-8 and consider your responses to each strategy. You may want to keep notes about your responses in a special book or journal.

Tips 1-4 ask you to consider what you believe

passion is and to identify what passion means to you. What role do you think passion should have in your life? Do you have any passion-blocking beliefs? What are your passion-building beliefs?

Tips 5-8 cover the consequences of ignoring your passion. How do you think not pursuing your dreams might affect you? How has it affected other people you know? What are your goals, hopes, and dreams for your future? What will having more passion in your life do for you?

1. WHAT IS PASSION?

"Nothing great in the world has been accomplished without passion."
G.W.F.Hegel, Philosopher

To be passionate is to be fully alive. Being passionate is a vital part of being human.

Passion is about emotion, feeling, zest and enthusiasm.

Passion is about intensity, fervor, ardor, and zeal.

Passion is about fire.

Passion is about eagerness and preoccupation.

Passion is about excitement and animation.

Passion is about determination and self-belief.

2. PASSION FOR ALL

"One person with passion is better than 40 people merely interested."
EM Forster, Writer

Every human being is capable of passion. But many people think they are not.

Remember, different people are passionate in different ways. Many people think that being passionate only means being loud or extroverted.

This isn't true at all. Many passionate people are shy or quiet or reserved. Passionate people come in all shapes, sizes, and ages. You can pursue your passion at any age and stage of your life.

What is true for you?

STEP 4: LIVE YOUR PASSION!

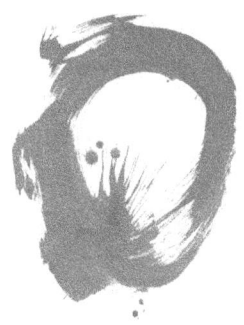

*T*ips numbered 27-40 in this section look at ways to help you inject more passion and purpose into your life.

Tips 27-28 look at passion beyond the world of work and the issue of achieving work/life balance.

Tips 29-33 look at some possible passion barriers. You'll be encouraged to consider any psychological issues that may need to be worked on so that you can fulfil your potential.

Where are you now and what do you want? What could stop you from doing the things you are passionate about? How could you live a more passionate life?

Tips 34-40 suggest strategies to maximise your success and overcome obstacles. How can you take greater responsibility for living a more passionate life? What will you need to do? What will you need to change?

1

DAILY TONIC

"Filling your own needs is not something that you do randomly, it's something that needs to be done on a regular basis."
Cassandra Gaisford, Author

Make passion a regular event. Do you regularly spend time doing things you enjoy? Can you do something every day to help keep your passion alive?

Only 15 or 30 minutes a day devoted to activities you love, and to those that move you closer to your dreams, can make a big difference to your health and happiness.

If finding the time or lacking energy is preventing you from doing more of the things you are passionate about, develop a strategy to restore the balance.

2

LIVING IN THE PASSION ZONE

"If you allow your fears to keep you from flying you will never reach your height."
India Arie, Singer

Why don't more people pursue their passions?

We have to try and live and work in the passion zone as much as possible. It sounds simple, but most people don't. Reasons vary and are numerous, some common ones include:

- Being caught in the comfort-rut
- Fear

- Lack of confidence and self-belief
- Procrastination

What, if anything, is stopping you from pursuing your passion?

Really analyse what holds you back and develop a strategy to overcome any obstacles that may stand in the way of you and your passion.

3
FEAR OF FAILURE

"I'd rather be a failure at something I love than a success at something I hate."
George Burns, Comedian

*I*n our Western culture, we often spend more time thinking of ways we could fail rather than ways we could succeed.

People also don't give themselves permission to make mistakes or to learn.

When was the last time you tested your fears?

If you felt the fear and did it anyway what's the worst that could happen?

. . .

Look for and collect examples of people who have turned "failure" into success.

4
FEAR OF SUCCESS

"It is our light, not our darkness, that most frightens us. We ask ourselves, who am I to be brilliant, successful, talented and fabulous? Actually, who are you NOT to be? Your playing small doesn't serve the world."

Marianne Williamson

Some people don't pursue their potential because they're afraid of success. Success can bring unwanted attention, criticism and the risk of failing.

Success can also be threatening to others who

haven't achieved their potential – even your best friends can become your worst critics.

Are you afraid of standing out? Are you prepared to be a tall poppy even though others may seek to cut you down? How could your success inspire others?

5
FEAR OF CHANGE

"Unless we try to do something beyond what we have already mastered we cannot grow."
Ronald Osborn, Writer

People often put more energy into resisting change and preserving the status quo than they do in embracing change.

Changing can be hard work. It means taking a risk and stepping into the unknown. Some people fear change because they believe they may lose what they have—even though what they have may be nothing at all.

For many people change means taking responsibility and ending years of blaming others, being a victim, or living in denial or in a state of apathy.

· · ·

How can you be empowered and confront your fears safely?

6

FEAR OF DISAPPOINTMENT

"You can't possibly net the prize if you're thinking about all the possible ways you can miss."
Cassandra Gaisford, Author

Some people die with their music still inside. They opt to cling to the hope of their aspirations rather than the reality of a possible disappointment and the risk of a shattered dream.

What's worse—the disappointment of a few setbacks, or the disappointment of a life spent unfulfilled and filled with regret?

. . .

ALL LIFE ARISES out of choice. What choices are you making now?

7

ALLOW NO DOUBT

"Winners are too busy to be sad, too positive to be doubtful, too optimistic to be fearful, too focused on success."

Cassandra Gaisford, Author

Attitude is everything. Be a guard for your words, thoughts, and feelings. Don't let self-doubt be the thing that pops your balloon.

Be your biggest fan. Back yourself 100%. We all have doubts, but it's amazing how your doubts will disappear once you are doing the things you love.

. . .

ARE you your biggest fan or worst enemy? How can you stay positive, confident and optimistic?

8

VISUALIZE YOUR PREFERRED FUTURE

"I do not know how to distinguish between our waking life and a dream. Are we not always living the life that we imagine?"
Henry Thoreau, Philosopher

Visualisation is a powerful technique used by many successful business and sports people. See your way to success.

Try to visualise your preferred future by closing your eyes and imagining a time in the future 1, 5, or 10 years from now. What are you doing? Who is there? How are you feeling? Walk toward the future and look back to today. What steps did you take to get there?

IF YOU SPEND time imagining the future you want you have without even knowing it begun to make it happen.

9

MAKE A PASSION ACTION PLAN

"To accomplish great things, we must not only act but also dream; not only believe but also plan."
Antole France, Writer

Some people think that fate will take care of their future. But the winners in life know that failing to plan is planning to fail.

Written goals, with action points and time frames, are essential if you really want to achieve a more passionate life.

MAKE A PASSION ACTION PLAN. Do something every

day to help move you closer to your goal of leading a more passionate life.

Don't forget to tick off and celebrate your achievements along the way to reinforce feelings of success.

10

SEND YOUR CRITICS AWAY

"Keep away from people who try to belittle your ambitions. Small people always do that, but the really great make you feel that you, too, can become great."

Mark Twain, Writer

If you are steering towards having more passion in your life, people may be jealous or threatened and criticise you. Be passionate anyway!

Don't be put off by negative feedback. Don't wait for others to give approval to your life. Send your critics on a holiday.

Be brave. Be bold. Be firm. Be audacious. You'll soon conquer your fears and convince others.

WHO COULD you look to for inspiration, encouragement, and support?

DID YOU ENJOY THIS EXCERPT?

How to Find Your Passion and Purpose: Four Easy Steps to Discover a Job You Want and Live the Life You Love is available as an audiobook, paperback, hardcover and eBook from all good online bookstores. I

Or you may prefer to take my online course, and watch inspirational and practical videos and other strategies to help you to fulfil your potential —https://the-coaching-lab.teachable.com/p/follow-your-passion-and-purpose-to-prosperity.

If you need more help to create a passion and purpose inspired business, *The Passion-Driven Business Planning Journal:The Effortless Path to*

Manifesting Your Business and Career Goals, available as a paperback and eBook will help. Available from all good online bookstores.

ACKNOWLEDGMENTS

My sincere thanks to Melinda Hammond for her super inspiring podcast
—https://writerontheroad.com.

Listening to her interview with fellow author Renee Conoulty motivated me to write this book.
I am truly indebted. You can listen to this interview here— https://writerontheroad.com/153-how-to-narrate-your-novel-with-renee-conoulty/

Thank you also to my fabulous illustrator and designer Steven Novak for making my vision a reality. As a child I always dreamed I had a flying carpet—and now I do, I really do!

And dear reader, thank you for purchasing my book and allowing me to inspire you.

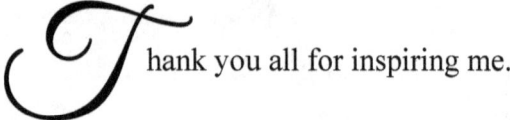hank you all for inspiring me.

ABOUT THE AUTHOR

CASSANDRA GAISFORD, is best known as *The Queen of Uplifting Inspiration.*

A former holistic therapist, award-winning artist, and #1 bestselling author. A corporate escapee, she now lives and works from her idyllic lifestyle property overlooking the Bay of Islands in New Zealand.

Cassandra's unique blend of business experience and qualifications (BCA, Dip Psych.), creative skills, and well-ness and holistic training (Dip Counselling, Reiki Master Teacher) blends pragmatism and commercial savvy with rare and unique insight and out-of-the-box-thinking for anyone wanting to achieve an extraordinary life.

ALSO BY THE AUTHOR

Stories and Fairytales

The Little Princess
The Little Princess Can Fly
I Have to Grow
The Boy Who Cried
Jojo Lost Her Confidence (written as C.G. Ford)
Lulu is a Black Sheep (written as C.G. Ford)

Non-fiction Self-Empowerment Books

Mid-Life Career Rescue
How to Find Your Passion and Purpose
Bounce: Overcoming Adversity, Building Resilience and Finding Joy
Anxiety Rescue: How to Overcome Anxiety, Panic, and Stress and Reclaim Joy
Boost Your Self-Esteem and Confidence
No! Why 'No' is the New 'Yes'

Leonardo da Vinci: Life Coach
Coco Chanel: Life Coach
How to Find Your Joy and Purpose
The Happy, Healthy Artist
Stress Less. Love Life More
Mind Your Drink: The Surprising Joy of Sobriety

and more…

More of Cassandra's practical and inspiring books on a range of life enhancing topics can be found on her website (www.cassandragaisford.com) and her author page at all good online bookstores.

Many titles are now available in audio.

STAY IN TOUCH

Follow Me and Continue To Be Supported, Encouraged, and Inspired

Subscribe to my newsletter and follow me on BookBub (https://www.bookbub.com/profile/cassandra-gaisford) and be the first to know about my new releases and giveaways

www.cassandragaisford.com
www.facebook.com/cassandra.gaisford
www.instagram.com/cassandragaisford
www.youtube.com/cassandragaisfordnz
www.pinterest.com/cassandraNZ
www.linkedin.com/in/cassandragaisford
www.twitter.com/cassandraNZ

And please, do check out some of my videos where I share strategies and tips to stress less and love life more—http://www.youtube.com/cassandragaisfordnz

BLOG

Subscribe and be inspired by regular posts to help you increase your wellness, follow your bliss, slay self-doubt, and sustain healthy habits.

Learn more about how to achieve happiness and success at work and life by visiting my blog:

www.cassandragaisford.com/archives

SPEAKING EVENTS

Cassandra is available internationally for speaking events aimed at wellness strategies, motivation, inspiration and as a keynote speaker.

She has an enthusiastic, humorous and passionate

style of delivery and is celebrated for her ability to motivate, inspire and enlighten.

For information navigate to www.cassandragaisford.com/contact/speaking

To ask Cassandra to come and speak at your workplace or conference, contact: cassandra@cassandragaisford.com

NEWSLETTERS

For inspiring tools and helpful tips subscribe to Cassandra's free newsletters here: http://www.cassandragaisford.com

Sign up now and receive a free eBook to help you find your passion and purpose!
http://eepurl.com/bEArfT

COPYRIGHT

Copyright © 2019 Cassandra Gaisford
Published by Blue Giraffe Publishing 2019

Blue Giraffe Publishing is a division of Worklife Solutions Ltd.

Cover Design by Steven Novak

All rights reserved. No part of this publication may be reproduced, distributed, or transmitted in any form or by any means, including photocopying, recording, or other electronic or mechanical methods, without the prior written permission of the author or publisher, except in the case of brief quotations embodied in reviews and certain other non-commercial uses permitted by copyright law.

Neither the publisher nor the author are engaged in rendering professional advice or services to the individual reader. The ideas, procedures, and suggestions contained in this book are not intended as a substitute for psychotherapy, counselling, or consulting with your physician.

The intent of the author is only to offer information of a general nature to help you in your quest for emotional, physical, and spiritual well-being.

Any use of information in this book is at the reader's discretion and risk. Neither the author nor the publisher can be held responsible for any loss, claim or damage arising out of the use, or misuse, of the suggestions made, the failure to take medical advice or for any material on third party websites.

ISBN PRINT: 978-0-9951138-2-4
  ISBN EBOOK: 978-0-9951138-1-7
  ISBN HARDCOVER: 978-0-9951138-8-6

First Edition

www.ingramcontent.com/pod-product-compliance
Lightning Source LLC
Chambersburg PA
CBHW020300030426
42336CB00010B/843